# *Subaru*
# *Impreza Turbo*

## *Andy Butler*
**PMM Books**

First published 2006


ISBN 09545579 8 0

PMM Books, an imprint of Peter Morgan Media Ltd.
PO Box 2561, Marlborough, Wiltshire, SN8 1YD, Great Britain.
Telephone: +44 1672 514038
E-mail: sales@pmmbooks.com
Website: www.pmmbooks.com

# Ultimate Buyers' Guide
## Subaru Impreza Turbo
# Contents

Subaru Impreza Turbo

# Introduction

Welcome to the intriguing, confusing and utterly addictive world of the Subaru Impreza Turbo.

This Ultimate Buyers' Guide will help you to identify and buy an Impreza Turbo, from the first versions built in 1992 and only available in the UK as grey imports, right up to the newest New Age Imprezas being built in 2005.

The guide includes facts and figures, year by year changes, some details on special models, as well as information on equipment and options that were available.

The buying section tells you what to look for when viewing an Impreza and gives invaluable tips on how to choose between the various models to get the right one for you.

The Impreza is one of a new breed of supercar that packs a mighty punch, handles fantastically well, and does it with up to five people on board. There's even an estate version that can travel almost as quickly, but do it with shopping, too!

Although many people aren't aware of it, the Impreza is a design that draws on Subaru's long history of cutting-edge four-wheel-drive technology. They made the first regular passenger car with all-wheel drive back in 1972 and have been gaining experience in getting the best performance out of the system ever since.

Launched in 1992, the first Impreza Turbos soon made a name for themselves amongst motoring enthusiasts, and the word spread wider when Imprezas went rallying in late 1993. By 1995 Colin McRae and Subaru had won their respective WRC titles, and Subaru retained the manufacturer's title for the next two years.

Over the next five years the Impreza's following grew as more people found out about the car's abilities, and the rally cars kept winning events. There were minor revisions of spec from year to year, and various special editions were launched through the model's lifespan, before the New Age Impreza arrived in 2000.

The major change was the body styling, but it was such a radical departure from what the public had been used to, it's fair to say it wasn't very well received. Help was at hand in 2003, when the bug-eyed Impreza was superseded with something far more palatable.

This new version is the one in production at the time of writing, and it looks to have saved Subaru's Impreza from an ignominious fate brought on simply by being stylistically challenged.

We hope that you find this guide entertaining and useful, but if you are unsure that your prospective Impreza purchase is indeed a wise one, have it checked out by one of the numerous Subaru specialists who have evolved to keep the car in tiptop condition.

Andy Butler
Deepest Cumbria
England

# Timeline for the Impreza Turbo

**November 1992**
Impreza WRX saloon released in Japan with 240PS (237bhp or 174kW) engine. An instant classic!

**October 1993**
1994 Model Year (MY) WRX is introduced with amended ECU programming, better electrical equipment and revised spring and damper tuning. Five-door WRX estate launched with 220PS motor.

**January 1994**
Subaru Technica International (STi) variant of WRX arrives with 250PS, reworked suspension and brakes, close-ratio gear kit, and various body alterations.

**March 1994**
Britain received first turbocharged Imprezas, simply badged as Impreza Turbo 2000.

**June 1995**
Series McRae is first UK special edition. Only available in Rally Blue mica with 16in Speedline Safari alloys, Recaro interior and factory fitted sunroof. Just 200 produced to celebrate Colin McRae's successes in WRC. He won championship later that year.

**October 1996**
Impreza restyled for 1997 MY to give more aggressive front end with sharper-looking nose and headlights. Both the bonnet vents and intercooler scoop revised. Engine work focused on eliminating turbo lag, using modified inlet tracts, and smaller turbo. UK models also received better seats.

**April 1997**
Catalunya is second UK special edition, released to celebrate winning Rally of Catalunya and second WRC Manufacturer title in 1996. Finished in black Mica with gold wheels, it had black and red interior, and air conditioning. Again, only 200 built.

**October 1997**
Major interior revisions see new dashboard and instrumentation, twin airbags and Momo steering wheel, plus improved trim. Exterior mods limited to upgrade to 16in alloys.

**March 1998**
Wide-bodied 22B rally replica released to celebrate Subaru's 40th anniversary. Two-door coupé with 2.2-litre turbocharged engine, 22B was only produced in Sonic Blue with 17in gold alloys. Initially only 400 were produced for Japan.

The early Impreza 2-door saloon looked too restrained to be a serious opponent to something as lairy as an Escort Corsworth – but it was!

### April 1998
Third UK special edition, Terzo, released to celebrate Subaru's third consecutive WRC Manufacturer title. 333 produced in metallic blue, with obligatory gold wheels, and Alcantara-trimmed interior equipped with air conditioning.

### October 1998
Impreza turbos get revised front bumper and medium level spoiler at rear. Power increased from 208 to 211bhp and brakes changed to four-pot calipers from STi models.
UK-spec 22B displayed at NEC Birmingham Motorshow. Only 16 were imported, with conversion to UK specification by Prodrive.

### April 1999
RB5 is fourth UK special edition. Blue Steel metallic paint and graphite-coloured Speedline 17in alloys, Alcantara trim and air con are standard. 444 produced to celebrate Richard Burns rejoining Subaru's WRC Team.

### October 1999
Further interior revisions along with new 16in alloys, colour-coded mirrors and door handles denote 2000 MY version.
Impreza P1 announced at London Motorshow. Only available in Sonic Blue with suspension and body styling by Subaru's rally partners, Prodrive.

### April 2000
Japanese-only STi S201 aero-bodied car is most wild-looking Impreza made. Engine mods produced 300PS power output. Only 300 were made as final Classic Impreza.

### October 2000
Ovoid-eyed New Age Impreza is launched worldwide in October 2000 (and receives an underwhelming reception!). Top version in UK is WRX 2.0-litre turbo, available in 4 and 5 door. STi unveiled in Japan.

### January 2001
USA and Canada see first turbocharged WRX at Detroit Motor Show.

### May 2001
UK's first New Age Impreza special edition released. UK300 comes in blue metallic with gold OZ 18in alloys, has  Prodrive front and rear spoilers, modified headlights and Alcantara trim. Only 300 produced.

**February 2002**
New WRX STi Type UK means genuine STi Impreza is finally available through Subaru UK. 265PS, six-speed gearbox, big Brembo brakes, new suspension and new headlights to improve bug-eyed looks.

**May 2002**
Subaru released several limited editions in Japan to celebrate 30th anniversary, including S202 - first Impreza to officially break unofficial 280PS power limit.

**September 2002**
Following huge criticisms over styling, face-lifted Impreza displayed at Paris Motorshow. Restyled from windscreen forward, front end is more appealing. Makeover and Bug-Eye headlights are no more.

**December 2003**
Subaru release Petter Solberg Special Edition in both STi and WRX format. Available in rally blue, STi is limited to 555 individually-numbered cars. WRX is also special edition, but with just V-Limited plate instead of individual numbering.

**January 2004**
Subaru UK announce WRX STi Type WR1, 320PS special edition with Driver Controlled Centre Diff, Ice Blue metallic paint and stainless steel grille inserts.

**October 2004**
Improvements for 2005 MY include major chassis revision with new inverted dampers.

**May 2005**
New Impreza WRX 300 has 265PS Prodrive Performance Pack and specially-badged interior trim. Only available in WR Blue with gold wheels, edition limited to 300 cars.

*The 2001 model Imprezas received a mixed reception for the new headlamp design*

X596 KOE

# Facts, figures and performance
## Classic Impreza, WRX STi Type R, STi 22B, 2001 and 2003 models

### Classic Impreza

### Bodyshell
4-door saloons and 5-door Sports Wagon estates

All-steel unitary construction, steel bonnet and bootlid (aluminium on WRX STi), glass fibre rear spoiler, 60-litre fuel tank

### Engine
Type EJ20 aluminium alloy, 1994cc liquid-cooled, four-cylinder, horizontally-opposed engine with five-bearing crankshaft. Four valves per cylinder operated by belt-driven double overhead camshafts per bank, IHI turbocharger with air-to-air intercooler, twin-catalysed exhaust system, electronic fuel injection and ignition control.

Bore and stroke: 92mm x 75mm
Compression ratio: 8.5:1
Maximum power: 237bhp (240PS or 174kW) at 6000rpm
Maximum torque: 304Nm (224lb.ft) at 5000rpm

### Transmission
Permanent 4-wheel drive with open front differential, and centre and rear viscous couplings. 5-speed manual gearbox (optional 4-speed automatic on WRX Sports Wagon)

### Suspension and steering
Front: MacPherson struts with coil springs, transverse link, anti-roll bar
Rear: MacPherson struts, coil springs, transverse link, lower trailing arms, anti-roll bar

Front track: 1460mm (57.5in)
Rear track: 1455mm (57.3in)
Power-assisted rack-and-pinion steering.

### Brakes, wheels, and tyres
Twin-circuit ABS-equipped system with servo assistance.
Front: twin-pot sliding calipers with 277mm ventilated discs
Rear: single-piston sliding calipers with 264mm solid discs
Alloy 6J x 15in wheels with 205/55/15 tyres (changed to alloy 6J x 16in wheels with 205/50/16 tyres from 1995 model year)

### Performance
0-60mph: 5.0 seconds (WRX Sports Wagon 5.1 seconds)
Top speed: 140mph

### Will it fit?
Length: 4340mm (170.9in)
Width: 1690mm (66.5in)
Height: 1435mm (56.5in)
Weight: 1230kg
Boot capacity: 353 litres

### WRX STi Type R, STi 22B differences

### Bodyshell
Both have stiffer 2-door coupé bodyshell. Extended wheelarches and seam-welding on 22B only

### Engine
Type 22B: EJ22 flat four
Capacity: 2212cc

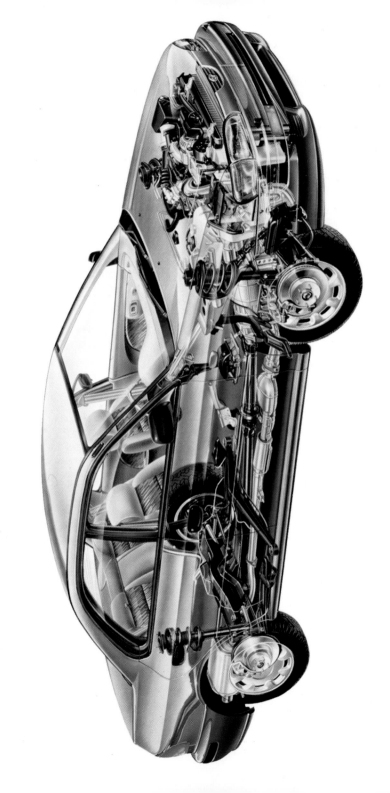

*Although this is the non-turbo G1 variant, you can clearly see the essnetial boxer-engine and four-wheel drive layout that has served the Impreza so well*

Bore x stroke (mm): 96.9 x 75mm bore
Maximum power: 276bhp (280PS or 202kW) at 6000rpm
Maximum torque: 360Nm (265lb.ft) at 3200rpm

**Transmission**
Type R uses Group N close-ratio gear kit, both Type R and 22B use Driver-Controlled Centre Differential (DCCD) and mechanical limited slip differential (LSD) in the rear

**Suspension and steering**
Bespoke forged aluminium arms on 22B to give wider track

**Brakes, wheels and tyres**
(F) Four-pot calipers and 292mm vented discs (R) Twin-pot calipers and vented discs, no ABS. 22B has larger rear discs and red-painted calipers.

**Performance**
0-60 mph: STi Type R 4.3 seconds; 22B 4.6 seconds
Top speed: STi Type R 130mph; 22B 140mph

## 2001 MY New Age Impreza WRX

## UK Spec cars: 4-door cars (5-door in brackets)

**Engine**
Maximum power: WRX 215bhp (218PS or 157kW) at 5600rpm
Maximum torque: 292Nm (215lb.ft) at 3600rpm
Three stage catalytic converter

**Transmission**
WR: 5-speed manual
STi: 6-speed manual

**Suspension and steering**
Steering speed sensitive power assisted rack and pinion

**Brakes, wheels and tyres**
Wheels 7J x 17in alloy all round
Tyres 215/45 ZR17 all round

**Performance**
Maximum speed: 143mph (140mph)
0-60mph: 5.9 seconds

**Will it fit?**
Length 4405mm, width 1730mm (1695mm), height 1440mm (1465mm), wheelbase 2525mm
Track front 1485mm (1460mm)
Track rear 1480mm (1450mm)
Ground clearance 155mm
Kerb weight 1385kg (1410kg)

## 2003 MY facelift Impreza WRX differences

**Engine**
Maximum power: 222bhp (225PS or 163kW) at 6500rpm
Maximum torque: 300Nm (221lb.ft) at 4000rpm

# *Impreza background*

When you consider that the Impreza was first launched in 1992, it's not immediately apparent that Subaru's history of four-wheel-drive vehicles goes back a lot further. In fact, the four-wheel-drive story almost goes back to the beginnings of the company, which only started producing vehicles in 1958. The strange 360 microcar didn't have any of the attributes we've come to expect from the Impreza, but everyone has to start somewhere!

The first recognisable element of the Impreza's design was the flat-four 'boxer' engine that appeared in 1966, and it is still unique amongst Japanese car manufacturers. This was used in a front-wheel-drive car known as the FF-1, and then powered the Leone series that surfaced in 1971.

The big news was the Leone 4WD Estate that was launched in 1972. This really was the world's first mass-produced four-wheel-drive car instead of just being a utilitarian off-roader. About the only other non, off-road four-wheel drive was the mid-1960s' Jensen Interceptor FF, but with its monster American V8 this could hardly be described as anything other than a bespoke high-performer.

So, the Leone brought a whole new level of traction and usability to the motoring masses, but it did it with regular car-like levels of user-friendliness. And while some farmers did drop their Land Rovers in favour of this 'proper' car that also handled slimy roads and tracks with aplomb, a whole new market opened up to Subaru. Soon, lots of customers who ventured away from tarmac roads for work or hobby began buying Leones, quickly elevating the unassuming Subaru to the rank of world's best-selling four-wheel-drive passenger car.

What Subaru didn't do was give the Leone a performance variant, and when the Audi

*Early Impreza 4-door saloon*

**Impreza Sports Special**
The facelifted Classic Impreza was given a more aggressive snout thanks to a new grille and bonnet

Quattro arrived in 1980 it showed that there was a place for a vehicle that was both high-performance and all-wheel drive. The Quattro's subsequent rallying successes proved there was a lot of sense in the combination, but it was 1989 before Subaru followed with a real high-performance alternative of their own. They did bring out a couple of turbocharged 4x4s before then, but the Leone variant was under powered and only available with an automatic transmission, and the XT sports coupé was, well, just plain odd.

Once the Legacy RS was launched, most of the design ideas that would go on to be used in the Impreza were brought into production. The EJ20 turbocharged all-alloy 2.0-litre boxer engine, the five-speed gearbox, four-wheel-drive system and front and rear suspension layouts would all be carried over into the new model.

Although Subaru did go rallying with the Legacy, its size meant it was bigger than ideal for throwing sideways down forest tracks and sliding through snow banks. The Impreza was designed to fill the hole in the range between the Legacy and the diminutive Justy.

After adapting the Legacy's floorpan to become the Impreza's foundation, the engineering team worked on the new car's shell to produce something stiffer but also lighter in weight. The suspension was thoroughly reworked, losing weight, increasing both its toughness and the wheel travel, and altering the geometry for a snappier response.

The flat-four motor was carried over direct from the Legacy, and it was such a good design with plenty of grunt – especially in turbo form – that it proved to be an ideal basis for a rally contender. The low weight,

Early Subaru interiors were a little lacklustre to say the least. This 1.8GL looked exactly the same as the Turbo apart from the steering wheel

and even lower centre of gravity when it was installed in the Impreza, both helped the way the car handled.

Further improving the car's on- and off-road abilities was the sophisticated all-wheel drive system that was Subaru's stock in trade. They had been developing this set-up for over two decades when the Impreza was first designed, so it was no surprise that it worked so well.

The key to the way the power was spread between the four wheels was the combination of an open front differential, with centre and rear viscous couplings. Under normal driving conditions, the power split was 50/50 front-to-rear. Subaru considered this optimal balance for most conditions, but when grip levels became variable, the central viscous coupling would sense which axle was losing traction, and divert power to the one that was still hanging on.

Although the front diff was a design that had no wheelspin-inhibiting mechanism, the two viscous couplings were seen as enough to control the power flow through the drivetrain. When the going became rough and loose, they apportioned drive to the wheels with grip, maximising drive and stability, and endowing the Impreza with the traction for which it has become famous. The system worked well on the road where surface contaminants could catch out a less-sophisticated chassis, but it was on a rally stage where it really proved its worth.

Launched initially on the Japanese market, the Impreza was soon a success. Everyone who tested the car raved about it, and the product of the Fuji Heavy Industries Yajima Factory became a sought-after vehicle. The first version released was the 237bhp (174kW) WRX saloon, which derived its name from the fact that it had been put together partly as a homologation vehicle for use in the World Rally Championship.

Within 18 months, a turbocharged Impreza had made its debut in Europe, but it wasn't the same car the Japanese had been enjoying. Producing 208bhp (153kW),

*The first Imprezas were an immediate success in Japan, and a turbocharged version made its debut in Europe in 1993*

*The early 5-door offered utility with practicality – and more than enough power to do the job!*

the European car ran with a smaller turbo and intercooler as well as a different engine management unit. At 100RON, Japanese fuel is a higher octane rating than that available throughout Europe, and Subaru didn't feel able to make the WRX motor run successfully on 95RON juice, so they detuned the EJ20 for the overseas market. It would be a long time before power outputs in Europe were on a level with Japan.

Another area where the rest of the world fell some way short of Japan was in the numbers of different Imprezas available. During their most prolific year, Subaru had 14 different versions for sale in Japan. There were two-doors, four-doors, five-doors, Type Rs, Type RAs, STis, V-Limiteds, manuals and automatics. The choice was bewildering,

but they all had slightly different reasons for being produced, and they all had a common bond – they were great cars to drive.

The basic layout of a flat-four motor and permanent all-wheel drive, both housed in a variety of practical body styles, has been the Impreza's trademark through three incarnations. After the first design lasted from 1992 until 2000, the new model arrived looking surprised and weird and, after only three years, it was superseded by an Impreza that was all new from the windscreen forward. The car's dynamic abilities were just as good, but that bug-eyed front end just didn't become part of the family. The new version has rescued the Impreza's fortunes, and looks like it will be here for some years to come.

**Impreza UK300**
the first 'New Age' special edition

## Model changes year by year

On its 1992 introduction, the Subaru Impreza was designed to fill the gap between the tiny Justy and the much larger Legacy, a job it did admirably. Probably because it was launched at the same time as everything else in the range, the 2.0-litre turbocharged WRX might have seemed a bit lost for attention at first. But it didn't take long before the buzz began to grow, and soon it was the only model everyone wanted to know about.

Over the ensuing years the Subaru designers and engineers have tried to refine and perfect the original design, rather than chase different goals and bring us a new car that is an Impreza in name only. This continuous development has lead to some of the finest on and off-road competitive machinery available in motorsport and to the enthusiastic road driver. This is how they tweaked it year on year.

The time references used throughout this chapter (and elsewhere) often refer to the automobile industry's model years, rather than a conventional calendar year. For instance a 1999 model refers to the time period 1 August 1998 to 31 July 1999.

### Bodyshell

For such a groundbreaking supercar, the Impreza Turbo didn't exactly set the pulse racing with its wild cutting-edge styling. In truth, the turbo did look more serious than the lowly, almost painfully bland normally-aspirated versions. A deeper front spoiler, large spotlights, a vented bonnet with large air scoop, side skirts and a rear spoiler all helped boost the car's visual appeal, but it still looked a lot more staid than something

*The basic Impreza shape is apparently based on the silhouette of a waterfowl in flight. Well, now you mention it, it's obvious...*

*Devoid of spoilers, the base Impreza wagon is a slightly odd proposition. No wonder the Turbo versions were so popular*

like an Escort Cosworth.

Under the surface, the Impreza had a few tricks that were designed to improve the bodyshell's performance, with some models having a solid rear bulkhead behind

*Subaru front grille badge*

the rear seat. It might not sound like much, but having this piece of steel bracing the rear of the shell where the suspension loads arrive did help to alleviate some twisting and flexing. It did cut down the vehicle's usability somewhat, meaning the fold-down rear seats couldn't be fitted, but in a sports saloon, this wasn't seen as a problem. Of course, the Sports Wagon was a regular estate layout inside. As it was never destined to be a competition vehicle this was of less concern, but enthusiastic drivers would notice the difference between variants.

When the first major redesign came along at the end of 1996, the Impreza took on a slightly more aggressive appearance with a redesigned front end. The headlights were slightly more-square, and the bonnet was reworked with new grilles and intake scoop. The changes were subtle, but the effect was very noticeable. At the rear end was a new

*With its fat wheelarches and exhuberant rear spoiler, the 22B was the nearest you could get to a rally Impreza on the road*

bumper design and high-level brake light incorporated into the spoiler.

UK-spec spoilers on Turbos were a much more restrained affair in comparison to the Japanese models, of which the 1994 STi's rear wing was incredibly tall. A mid-height spoiler sufficed on the rest of the range until the STi Version V WRC-lookalike spoiler arrived. The 22B also had a large rear wing with an adjustable blade to alter downforce.

Although the saloon and Sports Wagon share lots of common dimensions, with the rear seats up and the load cover in place there was a scant three litres' extra capacity in the five-door. In fact, very early tests even thought the saloon had a little more useable space. Of course, once the rear seats were flopped forwards the Wagon became much more capacious, with over three times the load space of its four-door cousin.

The big news came in 2000 when the New Age Impreza was launched. Most Impreza fans will remember this one for its 'interesting' styling, dominated by those ovoid front light units. No matter how much Subaru told the world that they were distinctive, dynamic,

*These triple-pack headlights went some way to masking the ugly frontal aspect of the New Age Impreza*

2005 Impreza WRX

higher performance, and so on, most people just thought they looked weird.

Happily, once they got behind the wheel, they found the car had been improved all round. A new bodyshell allowed Subaru – who had been working on this replacement car since 1997 – to engineer in lots more rigidity to the shell without significantly increasing the overall weight. The result was a shell that was 185 per cent better at resisting twisting, and 250 per cent better at resisting bending. These figures fell to 122 and 239 per cent for the estate version but whichever way you looked at it, the basis of the new chassis was superior. If only the same could be said of the exterior.

The STi Type R went further and used a seam-welded bodyshell to improve stiffness even more.

For another two years Subaru maintained they'd got the styling right. The new car really was distinctive. It had presence. They were adamant everyone would get used to it, right up to the point when they changed the front end again in 2003. Even if no-one ever admitted they were wrong, they proved it with the quick redesign. The new snout was much more appealing, and Subaru enthusiasts breathed a sigh of relief – we've even talked to people who finally changed from their Classic Impreza to the 2003 model because they simply couldn't face owning the 2000 version.

### Equipment and accessories

Although the Impreza Turbo was something of a performance bargain in the UK, undercutting the direct competition like

*They might look similar, but the rally car and its road going cousin are only related by their basic component layouts*

the Escort Cosworth by around £5000 in 4-door form, it missed out on a few choice accessories that were standard fitment for the Japanese market. The main deleted item was climate control, which turned into a cost option instead. Apart from that, the extras list was comparatively short – like on a lot of other Japanese cars.

From a buyer's perspective, this made things a little easier than if you were, say, hunting for a German sports car. Their accessory lists are generally so long and involved, you have to check which accessories are fitted before you can decide how realistic the price is.

With Japanese-spec Subarus, the equipment list is quite comprehensive, with climate control, electric windows and

electrically adjusted and folding mirrors topping things off. The stripped out RA versions are aimed at motorsport and dispensed with foglamps, audio, climate control underseal, electric windows and lots of sound deadening to help lose weight. But if you are looking at buying one of these, the omissions just prove what a hard-core car you've bought.

New Age Imprezas also had their RA version, and it too threw out the fripperies in an effort to drop kilos. It wasn't the most extreme lightweight though, because when the STi RA Spec C was released it had lost the front subframe, sound deadening, HID lamps, airbags and lots more. Weighing in 90kg less than a regular STi, the dieting obviously works.

*2005 Impreza WRX 300 limited edition*

The Impreza WRX STi Type UK interior is a colourful and comfortable environment from which to enjoy the car's towering performance

## Interior

At the car's 1992 launch, the quality of interior fixtures and fittings was best described as naff. As we mention in the Buying section, early dash plastics were poor and flimsy, door panels were cheaply finished, and the whole air was of something done on a miniscule budget.

Japanese domestic market vehicles did have better seats, but UK versions got slightly modified versions of cheapo saloon-car seats covered in tweed. They were neither comfortable nor grippy, and had no place in a car that could generate such immense accelerative and cornering forces.

In the UK, it wasn't until the Series McRae that the Impreza got decent seats, when Recaros were drafted in. At the 1996 facelift the Jap-spec seats started to be used in mainstream UK cars, so even if it wasn't a special edition, it was still more comfortable and supportive. With the 1997 model year interior mods, the main focus was to reduce noise levels, More sound deadening material

and a cloth headliner all helped improve the refinement.

The major interior facelift appeared in the 1998 model year cars with a new dash and instrumentation, better trim and door cards, and an airbag-equipped leather-trimmed Momo steering wheel. The handbrake and gear-knob also received leather trim, and the gearshift was swapped for one with a shorter throw.

When the New Age Imprezas arrived, the larger exterior translated into a little more interior room for the occupants. The control layout was praised for being less haphazard than the Classic Impreza's, and the materials used were all of a higher quality, making the car feel more luxurious. However, some thought the pursuit of refinement had lost something of the original car's ability to deliver a thrilling, involving drive. The 2003 facelifted cars use the same interior fixtures and fittings as the ovoid-eyed Impreza, so the feel of quality and being well screwed together remained.

*Impreza GX Sport interior*

*More purposeful dash on the 2005 Impreza WRX-STi Type UK*

The layout of the classic EJ20 horizontally-opposed 'boxer' engine. Compact, powerful and reliable – as long as it's serviced and tuned properly

## Engine

Throughout the Impreza's model life, the whole ethos has been one of progressive improvement, and this shows up best in the engine bay. Small mods netted small gains year on year and, although there was an unofficial agreement to limit power output to 276bhp (202kW), the torque figure kept creeping upward.

Initially the UK Turbo was a disappointment because it lagged behind the Japanese WRX to the tune of almost 30bhp – 208bhp (153kW) to 237bhp (174kW). It took until 1998 before the power was lifted to 215bhp (156kW). During that time torque had risen from 201lb.ft to 214lb.ft. (273Nm to 290Nm)

In 1996 Prodrive offered a Performance Package to raise a UK-spec. car's power to 237bhp (174kW) and give better torque – between 240lb.ft (325Nm) and 258lb.ft (350Nm) – by swapping the exhaust rear section and the air filter, and reworking the

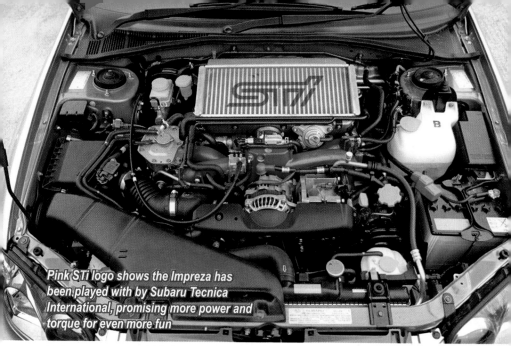

Pink STi logo shows the Impreza has been played with by Subaru Tecnica International, promising more power and torque for even more fun

engine management. This kit was improved in 1997 when it allowed the car to be run on regular unleaded fuel instead of Super.

When the P1 arrived, the UK market finally had a car that could compete with the power outputs of the Japanese Imprezas – while still passing UK emissions regs – with 276bhp (202kW) and 260lb.ft (353Nm) of maximum torque. It wasn't until 2004 that the UK-only WRX STi WR1 arrived with 315bhp (231kW) wrapped up in its limited-edition Ice Blue bodywork. This was the most powerful UK car until the New Age Impreza arrived – with the regular WRX only producing 215bhp (156kW) – and the WRX STi Type UK was fitted with a Prodrive Performance Pack to net 300bhp (220kW).

The Japanese had been playing with more powerful Imprezas since Day One, with the first WRX enjoying 237bhp (174kW) because of its bigger turbo and intercooler than the UK-spec cars. Even the Sports Wagon had 217bhp (159kW) at its launch. The WRX

STi enjoyed 247bhp (181kW) thanks to a blueprinted engine with stronger internals, an uprated turbo, bigger intercooler, freer-breathing exhaust and reprogrammed ECU. By 1995 the WRX saloon's motor was pumped up to 256bhp (188kW) - the Wagon remained at 217bhp (159kW) for now – but the STi had taken another leap and was now 271bhp (199kW).

During these power increases the torque figures were also rising, but not by the same sorts of big leaps as horsepower, and the STi was always produced a little more torque than its WRX counterpart. The only vehicle that gained power during the 1996 model year was the STi Wagon variant, which now boasted 256bhp (188kW), but it didn't stay like that for long.

For the 1997 model year, all the Imprezas except the Wagon were running 276bhp (202kW), so the only way to differentiate between the cars was the torque output. The STi Type Rs lead the way with 260lb.

ft (352kW), some way ahead of the WRX's 242lb.ft (328Nm). The regular WRX Wagons were even further behind at 224lb.ft (304Nm), and they had a horsepower deficiency of nearly 40bhp that they wouldn't make up before the Classic Impreza was withdrawn.

The 22B was also looked on as something of a disappointment because more power was expected from its enlarged 2.2-litre motor, which had been built using all the right bits. A roller-bearing turbo helped free the car from turbo lag, and new forged pistons and different fuel rails were welcome additions to the spec. Although power wasn't increased from 276bhp (202kW), torque was up to 264lb.ft (358Nm).

The Japanese WRX and 20K, as the Wagon was now known, started off with 247bhp (181kW). This came as a result of a bigger turbo and intercooler than the export models. The WRX STi continued with 276bhp (202kW), but torque had risen again to 275lb.ft (373Nm). A bigger turbo

and remapped ECU were the reasons for the increased oomph. In 2002, the S202 edition was a special based on a Spec. C Impreza, but with new ECU programming, silicone intake plumbing, and a performance exhaust. It gave a maximum power of 315bhp (231kW). In 2005 the S203 used the same motor to good effect in the facelifted car.

## Transmission

Of all the Subaru's ancillaries, the gearbox is the one that takes the most brickbats. Stories abound of gears stripping and synchros getting chewed up, and it's true that if the engine is tuned much above standard and the car's driven hard, the gears are a bit fragile.

Introduced with a 5-speed 'box, the Impreza kept this number of ratios through most of its model life, and only saw a 6-speeder in the New Age STi and STi Type UK cars, launched in 2000 and 2002 respectively.

*The Impreza only graduated to a six-speed gearbox with the 'New Age' STi and STi Type UK models*

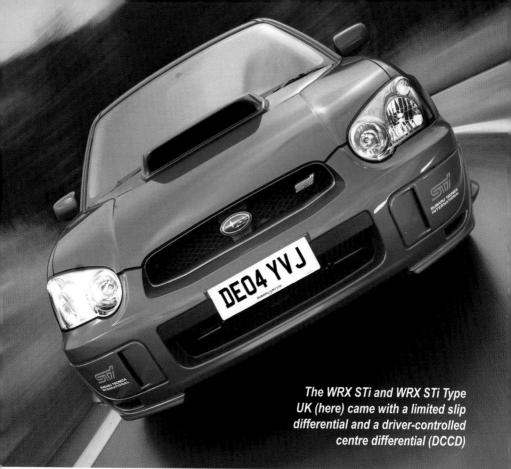

*The WRX STi and WRX STi Type UK (here) came with a limited slip differential and a driver-controlled centre differential (DCCD)*

Gear ratios were more subject to change, with the WRX STi getting a close-ratio gearset to help keep the engine on the boil in point-and-squirt motoring. The STi Type R cars had even closer ratios in their genuine Group N gearboxes, meaning top gear was only good for 19mph per 1000rpm. Talk about busy cruising!

The rest of the transmission consisted of an open front diff and viscous coupling centre and rear diffs, using a 50/50 torque split front-to-rear. This system worked throughout the range until the STi RA came along with its driver-controlled centre diff, and mechanical limited slip differential (LSD)

in the rear. The driver controls allowed the centre diff to be locked in a 50/50 split for use on really bad surfaces, or to go to 36/64 front/rear with the diff apportioning power to where the best traction was. Coupled to the mechanical rear LSD, it meant power oversteer was available in an Impreza for the first time.

New Age (2001 model) versions of the WRX STi and WRX STi Type UK were fitted with limited-slip front diffs and the driver-controlled centre diff (DCCD), and highly praised for their steering and cornering prowess, which was improved over cars that had no means of limiting front wheel spin.

## Suspension and steering

The Impreza's layout – MacPherson struts all round with lower control arms and an anti-roll bar at the front, and trailing arms and an anti-roll bar at the rear – was directly inherited from the Legacy RS, and the way it was integrated and set-up gave the Impreza generally fine handling. The low-slung motor helped lower the car's centre of gravity, but its far-forward position did contribute to some understeer.

The layout was almost the same as used in the other Impreza models, but the springs and dampers were uprated, and the anti-roll bars were new additions. For export, the springs were softened and the anti-roll bars were made from thinner stock, but the dampers were the same rating.

When the WRX STi surfaced in 1994, the suspension had been reworked, with the main change being die-cast aluminium lower arms that saved a significant amount of weight. A carbon-fibre strut brace also appeared in the STi, which ran with stiffer springs and dampers to sharpen the car's responses.

When the 22B was wheeled out in 1998, the suspension had been redesigned and the bodyshell grew huge wheelarches. The front and rear track grew as new forged aluminium arms joined up with uprated bushes and rose-jointed lateral links, and the Eibach springs and Prodrive-badged Bilstein dampers were the stiffest yet used on an Impreza.

When the New Age cars arrived the suspension used the same design, but the improvements to chassis stiffness helped suspension performance. Mountings were stronger, and minor geometry revisions

were made to take the handling up another notch. However, some pundits thought the responses from the new car weren't quite as good as the Classic.

The WRX STi and WRX STi Type UK both had further chassis improvements including inverted damper struts, that helped redress the situation. When the 2003 models were

*The 22B had uprated, wider track suspension - and the stiffest dampers yet used on an Impreza*

introduced, more work had been done to regain some of the lost sharpness, with sportier spring and damper rates being used on the WRX variant.

During these model variations, the steering system remained the same power –assisted rack and pinion design, but small geometry changes were introduced as suspension settings were changed, always with an eye to improving the steering feel, without making the cars too nervous. While most cars kept the 2.8-turns lock-to-lock gearing, the 22B and the New Age RA both used a 2.6-turn rack. This had been tried on the P1, but dropped by the designers because they felt it was too twitchy for UK driving.

### Brakes, wheels and tyres

At the 1992 launch, the Japanese Impreza WRX arrived with 6x15in rims and 205/55 rubber, so it wasn't exactly over-wheeled, and when the STi model was released in early 1994, it ran on the same wheel and tyre combination. This situation didn't last long though, because by October the 1995

*Early Imprezas ran on 15-inch alloy wheels*

model year cars were wearing new alloys with a diameter increased to 16in, with a tyre size amended to 205/55/16.

The next alteration was on the Impreza WRX STi Version II which added an inch to the width of the rim, and then ran with a 205/60/16 tyre. Bridgestone were the main rubber supplier, and various models of Expedia and Potenza were used depending on model. The next step up came with the awesome WRX STi Type R 22B which needed a 8.5x17in wheel and 235/40/17 tyre to fill its massive wheelarches.

In the UK, the wheel sizing was the almost the same with the Turbo starting on 15in rims in 1994 and then moving to 16in wheels for the McRae and Terzo special editions. The RB5 and P1 both used 7x17in rims shod with Pirelli P-Zero 205/45/17 tyres. For those who preferred the look of huge rims, at the expense of some ride quality, the P1 had an 8x18in option that required a 225/40/18 tyre.

Behind those wheels the Impreza ran a couple of brake types. Initial WRX cars came out with a twin-piston sliding caliper design clamping a ventilated disc for the front end, and a single-piston sliding caliper squeezing a solid disc for the rear. This was quite an effective set-up, but serious hotshoes demanded something better.

When the STi arrived it used 4-piston calipers over vented discs in front, and 2-piston calipers over vented discs at the back. These rear discs also found their way onto the WRX cars, too. Much stronger and more fade resistant, the STi also kept the WRX's ABS system. However, in 1995 the STi was only available as a stripped-down Type RA, and lost the ABS safety net.

For UK Subaru drivers there was a revision of the brakes in 1997, the better 4-pot calipers didn't arrive until the revision of the 1999 model year – until then they had to make do with the sliding calipers that were a design used for cost rather than performance reasons. The 22B had the same 4-pot front calipers as the regular STi – albeit painted red – but new rear calipers and discs to give it the best braking performance of the breed.

When the New Age Impreza arrived in the UK, it ran on 7x17in alloys accompanied by Bridgestone 215/45/17 tyres, and has stayed with this size as the standard option through to the new 2003-on facelifted cars. Japanese Imprezas used 6.5x16in alloys with a 7x17in option, while the STi versions also used 7x17in rims. There was also the choice to take the lightweight RA Impreza with 7x16in rims that saved a little more weight.

Displayed behind the new-style alloys, both UK and Japanese Imprezas wore Brembo 4-pot calipers and 294mm vented discs on their front ends, although the rear discs varied from Europe to Japan. Vented discs were used all round in Europe, but Japanese cars relied on solid rear discs. This set-up gave reassuring feel and performance for all but the fastest road work or trackday fun.

Perhaps the best stock brakes are to be found on the latest version of the WRX STi where the Brembo 4-pot front calipers are wrapped around 330mm vented discs. With immense power, fade resistance and a good feel at the pedal, they are the ultimate in factory anchors.

*Impreza RB5 special edition had 17-inch Speedline rally rims to complete the conversion*

*Gold finish for the 17-inch alloys on the Terzo*

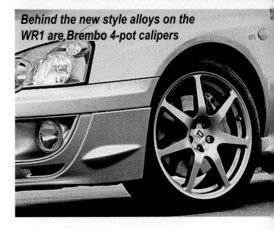

*Behind the new style alloys on the WR1 are Brembo 4-pot calipers*

1995's Series McRae was the first special edition in the UK. Continued rally successes would see Subaru introducing other low volume specials to celebrate consecutive World Rally Championships

# Special models

If there's one thing that Subaru's marketing department like, it's bringing out special versions of Imprezas to celebrate performance and competition milestones, and to puzzle anyone who isn't intimately familiar with the model options.

In the UK market there were four commemorative models, starting with the Series McRae launched in June 1995. This was built to celebrate Colin McRae's World Rally Championship (WRC) successes of the previous year, when he won the home RAC Rally. He would go on to even greater successes the following season, so bringing the special out mid-year seemed like someone had been crystal ball gazing.

Prepared by Prodrive near Oxford, the McRae was based on a Rally Blue Mica car with gold Speedline Safari wheels, and it had a pair of embroidered Recaro seats that told you who you were worshipping every time you got in. The car was a limited edition of only 200, starting at 01 and running to 201 so as to miss out number 13. The dash wore a numbered plaque to prove authenticity. An electric sunroof was a slightly strange option to include in the standard spec of a car that paid homage to a rally legend.

The next UK special edition was the Impreza Catalunya, named after the event that saw Subaru clinch the 1996 WRC constructors' title.

*1997 Impreza Catalunya*

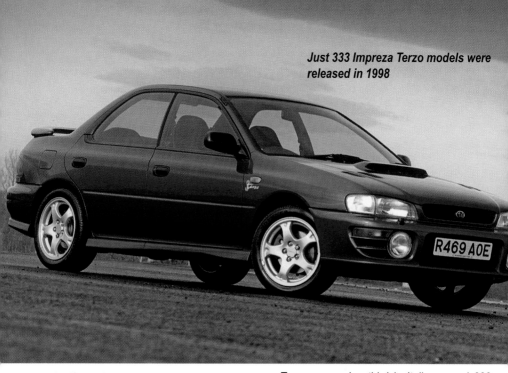

*Just 333 Impreza Terzo models were released in 1998*

McRae failed to retain his 1995 title, but the company was happy enough with their achievement to mark it in this way. The Cat, as it became known, arrived in March 1997, and was again limited to 200 vehicles.

Offered in sparkling black Mica paintwork, the accent colour was red, which turned up on the seats, interior trim and floor mats. The Catalunya badging was also red, but thankfully the 15-inch alloys remained in the tasteful gold seen previously. Other interior mods were a shorter rally-style gearlever, a carbon surround for the instruments, and air conditioning as standard.

It was only just over a year before the next UK special edition came out, and again it was produced to celebrate yet another rally world championship win for Subaru. Because it was the third win, the car was christened

Terzo – meaning third in Italian – and 333 cars were built.

The colour combo was back to the trusty blue with gold wheels, although the blue wasn't exactly the rally car hue, and the wheels had gone up to 16-inchers. Re-trimmed STi-style seats and panelling differentiated the interior, and air conditioning made it back onto the standard equipment list. As with the previous two specials, the Terzo also got a dashboard-mounted numbered plaque, but by my reckoning, the car was 66.5 per cent less exclusive than its predecessors.

Probably the best thought-of UK special was the final one offered on the Classic Imprezas. Launched in March 1999, the RB5 was a celebration of Richard Burns' return to the Subaru fold, using his initials and his race number. Based on a stiffer shell with a rear bulkhead and no folding-seat option, the Blue

*Best respected Classic Impreza is the 1999 RB5*

Steel metallic paint and pewter Speedline 17-inch wheels made it instantly recognisable.

You couldn't escape the RB5 logo that was displayed on the foglight covers, floormats and around the body, but standard features like the Prodrive quickshift and the Alcantara-trimmed cabin made the 444 examples built very desirable.

Prodrive's WR Sport Performance Package was a popular fitment to the RB5, boosting maximum power to 237bhp (174kW) and increasing maximum torque, particularly

*At Last! A UK Impreza with a decent rear spoiler!*

*1999 Impreza P1 by Prodrive*

*Engine bay of the Impreza P1*

*Attractive interior of the P1*

through the midrange, to 258lb.ft (350Nm).

Prodrive had been involved with Subaru's WRC rallying campaigns and providing performance upgrades for Scoobies for years. They offered Interior, Exterior and Driver Enhancement packages to suit individual owners' needs and, when all three packages were fitted at one time, the car received Prodrive WR Sport badging. On top of these there was a Performance Pack, but there wasn't one vehicle where it all came together in one unified package until the launch of the P1 in late 1999.

Subaru UK knew they weren't addressing the demand that was fuelling the grey import market to provide Imprezas like the STi Type R. The Prodrive One project was initiated to deliver a full Euro-friendly version with the same performance.

Mclaren F1 designer Peter Stevens was drafted in to pen the P1's spoilers and OZ alloy wheels, and the engineering team worked to make the STi Type R two-door car pass the EU regulations regarding noise, emissions, and crash testing. This last section was thought to be the easiest because the two-door shell was better than the four- and five-door cars already on sale.

Emissions work was more involved, requiring a more efficient single catalytic converter and a reprogramming of the ECU. The noise regs were slightly easier to pass because the P1 was fast enough to be tested under the Supercar regulations, which allowed a car to be one dB louder.

Finished in Sonic Blue, the P1 looked the part and performed well, although there were soon mumbles about the handling and braking under hard use. The answer came in the form of the P1 WR which ran on 18-inch OZ alloys with 225/35 Pirelli P Zeros Taking up residence behind the front wheels was a set of Alcon four-pot calipers and 330mm diameter discs that eliminated any worries about the car's brake performance at a stroke. Although the ride suffered because of the lower-profile tyres, the result was a more focused P1, closer in character to the Japanese import Type Rs.

On the Japanese scene there weren't the same number of commemorative models, but that didn't stop there being a flood of different Imprezas available. Apart from the mainstay WRX and WRX STi versions, there were the stripped-down Type RA cars that were better for use as foundations for motorsport use, as they were outfitted with better spec parts, and didn't carry any excessive weight. The Type R cars arrived as two-door coupés in 1998 - available as STis or V-Limiteds – and the 22B topped off the range in 1998.

The S201 was the final fling of the Classic

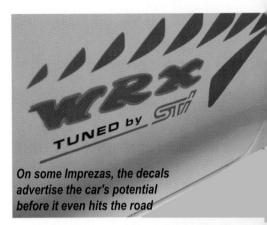

*On some Imprezas, the decals advertise the car's potential before it even hits the road*

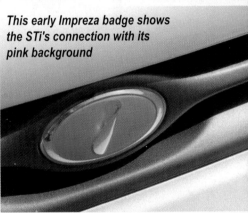

*This early Impreza badge shows the STi's connection with its pink background*

*The most sought-after badge to grace a Classic Impreza – the 22B*

An intercooler water spray was added in an attempt to improve the efficiency of the top-mounted intercooler

Driver adjusted centre differential allowed power-oversteer in an Impreza for the first time

C.DIFF

Interior of the 2005-model WRX 300

*2004 Impreza STi WR1 in Ice blue metallic*

Impreza shape, and a wild shape it was, too. Smoothed over with large aerodynamic add-ons, the S201 also had 296bhp (217kW) to keep it motoring. Only 300 were built, and most have remained inside Japan.

The S-series spawned the S202 when the New Age Impreza Spec C was tuned to provide 315bhp (231kW) in 2002, but it wasn't quite the outlandish be-spoilered affair that was the S201. An S203 arrived in 2005, based on the facelifted Impreza Spec C, and again used the reprogrammed ECU, silicon intake plumbing and less-restrictive exhaust to boost power to 315bhp.

*I preferred it when they drove Range Rovers and Ford Escorts...*

# Vehicle identification

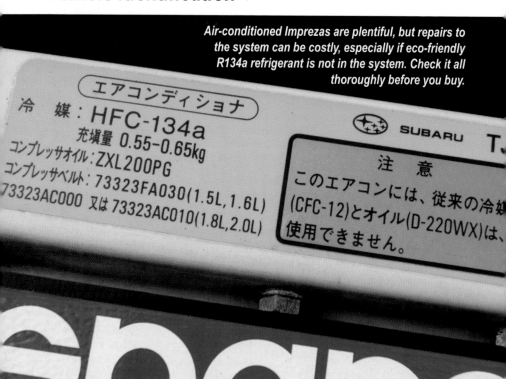

*Air-conditioned Imprezas are plentiful, but repairs to the system can be costly, especially if eco-friendly R134a refrigerant is not in the system. Check it all thoroughly before you buy.*

When you are looking at an Impreza, it's very important to check the chassis code and the 17-digit Vehicle Identification Number (or VIN) very carefully.

Firstly, you want to check that the code corresponds with the car you think you're buying, and secondly you want to establish that the car's VIN matches the car's chassis number that is shown on the registration documents.

The code and VIN can be found on the chassis plate within the engine bay. The VIN also appears on the rear firewall of the engine bay.

Here's a quick rundown on the codes used on the chassis plate.

Subaru employ a short seven-character code to identify their different Impreza models, and this is how it works:

First character - Model Code - G for Impreza (S for Forester, B for Legacy)

Second character - Body Type - C for saloon and coupé, F for Sports Wagon

Third character - Engine Type - 8 for EJ20 2.0-litre turbo (1 for 1.5-litre, 4 for 1.6-litre, 6 for 1.8-litre)

Fourth character - Year Series Code - A for Model Year 1993, B for MY94, C for MY95/96, D for MY97, E for MY98, F for MY99, G for MY2000, H for MY01, I for MY02, J for MY03, K for MY04, L for MY05

Fifth character - Door Option - 2 for two-door coupé, 4 for four-door saloon, 5 for five-door estate

Sixth character - Model Type - 8 for WRX, 7 for RA, E for STi (from Version III on), D for STi Type R and RA, S for 22B

Seventh character - Transmission type - D for five-speed manual, P for four-speed auto,

So, bearing these in mind, you can see that if your heart is set on a 1998 WRX Type R STi Version IV the code should be GC8E2DD, meaning Impreza, saloon or coupé, 2.0-litre turbo, MY98, two-door, STi Type R or RA, Five-speed manual transmission.

This lets you know that if you check the code against the VIN plate, and it doesn't line up with this layout, something is wrong. It's probably best to walk away because you're looking at a car that isn't what it purports to be, and you might be dealing with someone a little shady.

## Model codes from 2001 onwards

The 7 digit model codes for the 2001 onwards models are as follows: 1st digit refers to the series "G" = Impreza; 2nd digit refers to body style "D" = 4 door sedan, "G" = wagon; 3rd digit refers to engine displacement, drive system and suspension system: "4" = 1.6L FWD, "5" = 1.6L AWD, "9" = 2.0L AWD, "A" = 2.0L AWD turbo [WRX], "B" = 2.0L AWD high power turbo [STI], "E" = 2.5L AWD. The 4th digit refers to model year "E" = 2005MY; 5th digit refers to destination "K" = RHD, "L" = LHD; 6th digit refers to vehicle grade "3" = Base, "4" = TS, "5" = GX, "6" = RS, "7" = Outback, "8" = WRX, "E" = STi; the 7th digit refers to the transmission and fuel feed system.

"K" = sohc mpi dual range 5-speed manual transmission

"G" = sohc mpi 5-speed manual

"R" = sohc mpi 4-speed automatic transmission

"T" = dohc b mpi 4speed auto sport shift

"J" = sohc mpi 5speed manual awd

"D" = dohc b mpi 5speed manual awd

"H" = dohc b mpi 6speed manual awd

*One of the performance bargains available at the moment, a well-sorted Classic Impreza is good to look at, and even better to drive*

# Buying a used Impreza

## Introduction

Buying a used Subaru Impreza can be a bit of a daunting task, especially for someone who's not very technically minded. However, using the information here will help you find a diamond in the midden – as long as you look hard enough. Before we get stuck into the actual car info, here are a few words of advice.

Try and take a non-buying friend with you. Their cooling views might just stop you getting too carried away and buying something that you'd regret afterwards. Check out the seller as carefully as you check out the car. Scoobies are well built in the factory, but incorrect or missing maintenance will cost someone dearly further down the line.

An excellent way of making sure you end up with a good car is to drive as many of the type you want as you can. After a few test sessions, you'll have a good idea what they all feel like, how the car sounds when it's travelling, how the controls feel and so on. Unless you are incredibly lucky, don't buy the first Impreza you come across just because your heart says: 'This is the one, look at the colour!'

So, enough generalities, let's move on to spotting what goes pop on an Impreza.

## Grey import or UK Spec?

One of the main questions you have to ask yourself is whether you want a so-called grey import or a UK-specification car. Over the past few years various people have launched scare campaigns about the perils of buying an import, but as the industry has evolved, the worries are now down to minuscule levels – as long as you tread carefully.

The main complaint was the lack of history accompanying a car that came from an auction in Japan. Papers would be missing, you didn't get any servicing information, you couldn't validate the mileage, and so

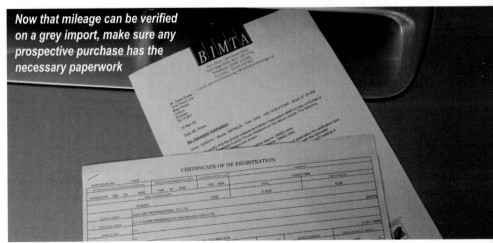

*Now that mileage can be verified on a grey import, make sure any prospective purchase has the necessary paperwork*

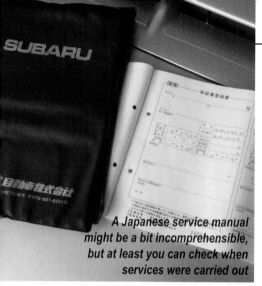

*A Japanese service manual might be a bit incomprehensible, but at least you can check when services were carried out*

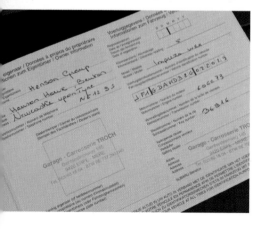

on. Today though, things are a little more organised. Respected import dealers now can provide proof of the mileage of the vehicle at the time of auction through a British Independent Motor Trade Association (BIMTA) scheme, and get a certificate to show it. This certification also proves the vehicle isn't stolen, and is free from any outstanding finance.

Also, the service and handbooks do come with the majority of greys. OK, you might not be able to read exactly what's gone on, but the pictorial service check sheets are often in the documentation, and the date and mileage are written in regular text, so you can see how often the car went for a check-up.

The last horror story used to be parts' availability, but now there are so many companies bringing in the specialist bits, even rare imports shouldn't be off the road for too long. Even the old bugbear of insurance is being eradicated as specialist insurers force mainstream companies to look at offering sensible quotes on what are often only slightly different versions of cars that have always been available here anyway.

Bearing in mind that the Japanese cars aren't subjected to winters of road salt, are often very well serviced, and their mileages can be quite low compared to those in the UK, the case for buying a grey import is very strong.

On the other side of the coin, a UK-spec car will have been supplied in the EU, have a factory warranty – the balance of which would transfer with the car if it was young enough – and shouldn't cause any difficulties if you need parts. It will also be more appealing to some of the official franchised dealer network, if you want to use them for servicing and repair work. There are still pockets of resistance among dealers who treat imports and their owners with a degree of contempt.

When it comes to actually looking at cars, the UK-supplied Imprezas are often less-well specified, and can also show the results of running on our salted winter roads. And there isn't the choice of specials that there is among those that come from Japan, with models like the Series McRae and RB5 attracting premiums because of their rarity.

## Documentation

One way of ensuring you are getting a genuine car is to get hold of the service information and make sure it all tallies up with the car you're looking at. Import cars used to be a lot harder to check but, as we've mentioned, BIMTA have been instrumental in lifting standards across the import industry.

Now, it's definitely possible to buy a car

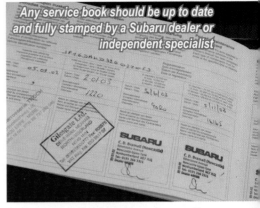

*Any service book should be up to date and fully stamped by a Subaru dealer or independent specialist*

that's just been imported from Japan with a guaranteed mileage certificate. And service history does come with a lot of Jap imports, even if it can be unintelligible. Of course, if you're buying a UK model, or a car that's been in this country for some time, there should be plenty of paperwork to go through, and all of it should easily align itself to the car in question.

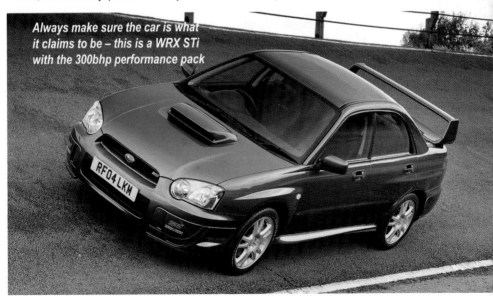

*Always make sure the car is what it claims to be – this is a WRX STi with the 300bhp performance pack*

*Huge rear spoiler on this WRX STi is a close replica of the rally car's downforce-inducing monster*

## Bodyshell

Before you go looking at the condition of the car, make sure it's actually what it purports to be. The chassis number is located on the strut tower, and should line up with the paperwork that's coming with the car. And never, ever buy a car without paperwork, regardless of the reasoning the seller gives for not having any. If you do and it turns out to be a car that's been nicked, then the car will be repossessed, you'll lose your money and vehicle and, in some cases, be prosecuted for handling stolen goods.

The main thing to look for on a UK car is badly-repaired accident damage. All vehicles sold in the UK are undersealed and treated with rust inhibitor so that just leaves poor workmanship as the main consideration.

You can check this by looking down the sides of the car for ripples, looking at shut gaps and panel fits for large or uneven gaps, and trying to see if there are any obvious marks under the paint. It's not easy on a rainy day, but in most light conditions you can find anything other than an exemplary repair. Structural steel can be more difficult to repair than exterior panelwork, so check out areas like the boot floor to make sure it's nice and flat.

Of course, the seller may be very up front about previous damage and have adjusted the price to suit. If this is the case, make sure you really want a car with some 'history' that might hamper you selling it at a later date. And be sure to check that the disclosed damage isn't a smoke screen concealing much worse horrors hiding under the surface. It has been known.

It isn't unusual for any car to have had paint these days, what with careless parking and stone chips eating away at body finishes all day long. If you do spot something has been blown in, ask awkward questions about what damage was under the paint repair and be prepared to walk away if you don't like the answers. There are plenty more Scoobies out there.

Japanese import cars are a little more involved than their UK-supplied cousins. This is because you have to check for the same sort of accident repairs and quality of workmanship as on a UK vehicle, but you also have to ensure that adequate undersealing and anti-stonechip coatings have been applied to the car to help it weather the unaccustomed road salt.

The area that can be worst affected is the edge of the wheelarch, where two sheets of steel meet, just out of sight. This edge can take a beating from debris thrown up by the tyre and, if the paint cracks off, rust starts chomping on the exposed metal. If you are buying a fresh import, get it properly sealed in this area to keep problems at bay.

### Equipment, trim and accessories

Unlike some other upmarket sports cars, Subaru Impreza values aren't slaves to the options list. Being Japanese, it was well equipped as standard, so hunting round for cars that have had all the toys fitted isn't really necessary. Certain models do miss out on some of the creature comforts, but this harks back to their stripped-out readiness

Damage to the lower front spoiler can indicate a car that has suffered very hard use, so check for scuffs and scrapes

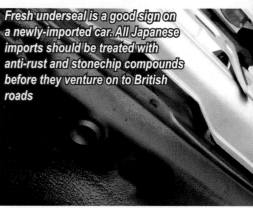

Fresh underseal is a good sign on a newly-imported car. All Japanese imports should be treated with anti-rust and stonechip compounds before they venture on to British roads

*Check this wheelarch seam for paint blemishes and rust brought on by stonechip damage*

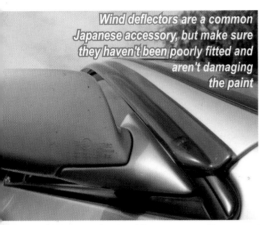

Wind deflectors are a common Japanese accessory, but make sure they haven't been poorly fitted and aren't damaging the paint

for getting involved in motorsport. If you want the lightest, fastest-reacting Scooby, one of these Type RA lightweights could be the very

thing you're looking for.

Obviously, you need to check that everything works, so have a few minutes playing with all the controls. Generally, Subaru electrics live up to the Japanese work ethic and are very reliable, and many faults are brought on through poorly added accessories. The only things to check carefully are the wiring to the headlamps, which is marginal at best and, if someone has fitted bigger headlight bulbs, a whole auxiliary loom is required to stop the standard one melting under the strain.

During your equipment check pay particular attention to the air conditioning – if fitted – and be sure it does chill the incoming air to freezing levels. Cycle the temperature

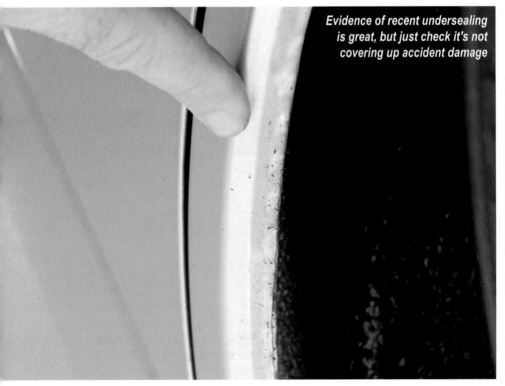

*Evidence of recent undersealing is great, but just check it's not covering up accident damage*

control up to hot and then down to cold, and work the fan through all speeds. If the blower works but you don't notice that the gale blowing through the vents drops from hot to very cold, you've got problems.

This could be either something simple and relatively cheap like an air-con re-gas, or expensive and involved like needing a new condenser or compressor. If you are buying from a dealer, get them to sort it out before you go ahead with the purchase, or price up repairs before you have a final haggle.

If you are considering a newly imported car, have a very good look at any accessories added by the previous Japanese owner. As we've mentioned, although any

*Additional gauges are often fitted by enthusiastic drivers. Be ready to check that they've been fitted and wired correctly*

*These STi badges are very expensive to replace, so make sure that none are missing if you're looking at a 22B*

*How did this get damaged? Definitely something to find out before money changes hands*

professionally-installed after-market bits should be fine, some of the DIY add-ons leave plenty to be desired in the wiring department.

*To convert Japanese KPH speedos to read MPH requires either this mechanical gearbox for the speedo drive or....*

UK-legal rear foglights need fitting to Japanese imports, and they should be fitted neatly like this

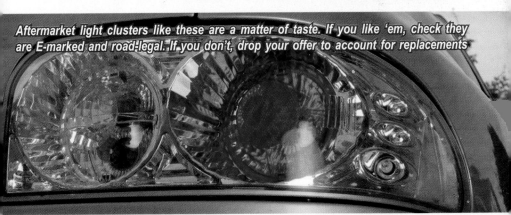

Aftermarket light clusters like these are a matter of taste. If you like 'em, check they are E-marked and road-legal. If you don't, drop your offer to account for replacements

...this electronic box of tricks. These devices delimit the car's top speed and stop it coughing and spluttering at 112mph (180kph)

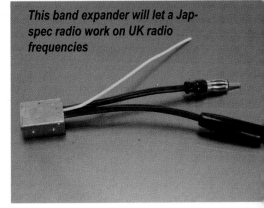

This band expander will let a Jap-spec radio work on UK radio frequencies

Stock Momo airbag steering wheel is much better than most airbaggers. Note the additional tacho on the dashboard – a possible addition by a boy-racer perhaps?

## Interior

In pre-October 1996 UK cars, the interior is bland. And that's being kind. Cheap plastics, unsupportive seats, naff carpet – nothing is particularly sought after. And the quality isn't too hot either, so expect sagging, worn out seats, scratched dash plastic, heel marks worn through the carpet near the pedals and so on. The poor design and quality of the earlier stuff is the main reason so many cars have after-market replacements fitted.

Changing the dodgy early trim for something in better condition is probably a non-starter from a financial standpoint, as well as the difficulty of finding replacement bits. However, fitting different seats and a new steering wheel might just make the interior bearable. It depends what you want the car for, and how much you are prepared to pay to bring it up to the spec. you want.

Post 1996 things improved tremendously, with all Imprezas getting better cloth trim, and the Turbos getting proper sports seats that went some way to locating a driver under the cornering forces the car could generate. The best interior trim levels were saved for the special versions like the Series McRae, Catalunya, Terzo and RB5, but the regular versions were now much more appealing places to be.

The Jap-spec cars were generally better-equipped, with niceties like electrically-adjusted mirrors that folded in at the push of a button. Seating was also better from the earliest examples, although they can wear to a shiny finish if the car has done a few miles.

Early UK Impreza Turbos had awful seating, even when it's in good condition

Japanese-spec seating – as in this photo – was much more supportive and in keeping with the car's performance potential. And they wear quite well too

Rear seating is remarkably practical

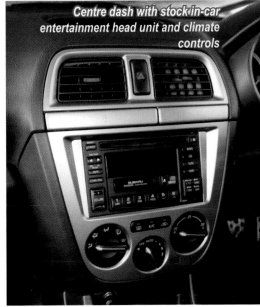

Centre dash with stock in-car entertainment head unit and climate controls

Here you can see the layout of the opposed-cylinder boxer engine and its DOHC per bank camshafts. This high performance motor also has the exhaust pipes lagged to help lower the engine bay temperature

### Engine

I suppose Subaru enthusiasts must get tired of reading this sort of comment, but the biggest problems an Impreza faces are inadequate maintenance and ill-considered performance tuning. If you are looking for an Impreza and find one that has missing service history, or the owner has 'done it all himself' be very wary.

It's not that servicing a Subaru is particularly more expensive than anything else, it's just that unless it is done by a trained technician - a main dealer or a specialist – things will get missed and engine longevity will suffer. Oil changes are of paramount importance on any turbocharged car, with Subaru's recommended oil and filter interval at 7500 miles (10,000 miles on the 2001-onwards cars). Changing the oil at half that interval would be a good idea if you drive your car hard.

While you're under the bonnet, remove the dipstick and look at the oil. It should be tinged with colour, but otherwise look clean. You can also rub a little between finger and thumb to see if it feels gritty or smooth.

Cambelt changes are vital to stave off major damage. The recommended interval is 36 months or 45,000 miles, whichever's sooner. Turbochargers are also prone to suffering from abuse, especially in the warm-up and cool-down phases of a trip. If you are buying privately, let the owner start the car and watch how he or she treats it for the first few miles.

Lots of throttle and savage use of the clutch and brakes might be impressive to some but, if the car hasn't warmed up, just

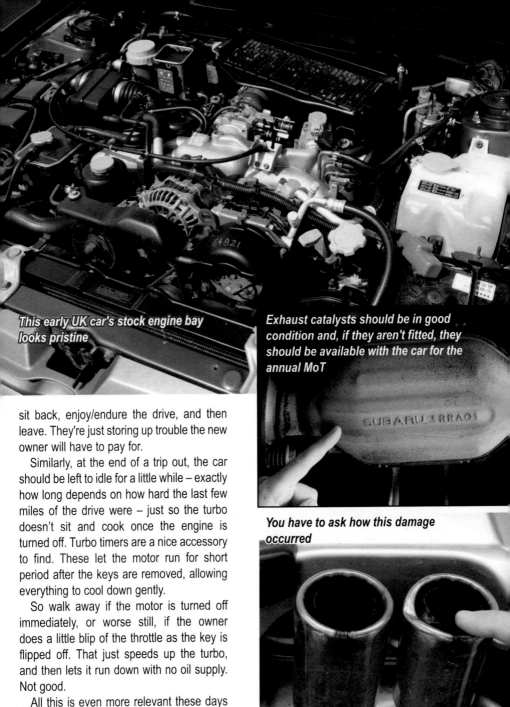

*This early UK car's stock engine bay looks pristine*

*Exhaust catalysts should be in good condition and, if they aren't fitted, they should be available with the car for the annual MoT*

*You have to ask how this damage occurred*

sit back, enjoy/endure the drive, and then leave. They're just storing up trouble the new owner will have to pay for.

Similarly, at the end of a trip out, the car should be left to idle for a little while – exactly how long depends on how hard the last few miles of the drive were – just so the turbo doesn't sit and cook once the engine is turned off. Turbo timers are a nice accessory to find. These let the motor run for short period after the keys are removed, allowing everything to cool down gently.

So walk away if the motor is turned off immediately, or worse still, if the owner does a little blip of the throttle as the key is flipped off. That just speeds up the turbo, and then lets it run down with no oil supply. Not good.

All this is even more relevant these days

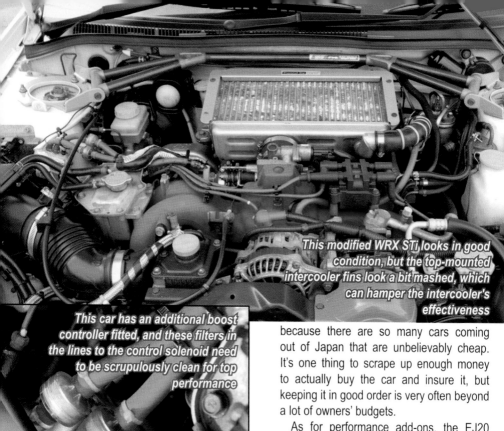

This modified WRX STi looks in good condition, but the top-mounted intercooler fins look a bit mashed, which can hamper the intercooler's effectiveness

This car has an additional boost controller fitted, and these filters in the lines to the control solenoid need to be scrupulously clean for top performance

This intercooler looks to be in good condition, without many damaged fins

because there are so many cars coming out of Japan that are unbelievably cheap. It's one thing to scrape up enough money to actually buy the car and insure it, but keeping it in good order is very often beyond a lot of owners' budgets.

As for performance add-ons, the EJ20 boxer engine is robust when the right mods are done in the right way. Simply winding up the boost and pouring more fuel in is a recipe for a short-lived hit of extra power, followed by a long period of misery as the engine is removed and rebuilt. So, beware of anything tuned unless you have conclusive proof it's been done properly.

As far as checking for faults goes, you should visually inspect for fluid leaks. This isn't a general problem, but if the motor has been apart and poorly rebuilt, you could see some weepage around the joints. If it all looks dry, start it up and have a good listen. The flat four motor sounds wonderfully gruff, but any untoward rattling and knocking should be investigated further. Some 1998 cars did suffer from piston slap problems, manifesting themselves as a knocking noise under 2000rpm, but these should have been sorted under warranty.

## Transmission

With over two decades of experience in all-wheel-drive systems, Subaru really knew what they were doing when they put the Impreza's transmission together. Its 50/50 torque split alters almost instantaneously when road conditions dictate, and the grip levels can seem astonishingly high.

As for faults, the gearbox can be a little soft, and bearings and synchros can fail after surprisingly short mileages if given hard use. During the test drive, check that every gear engages smoothly, and that there are no nasty whines and grumbles from the 'box, particularly on overrun.

While we have known clutches to last over 40,000 miles, it's not unusual for a car that's been thrashed to eat a clutch much

quicker. Juddering while the engine is cold is quite normal, but if the judders are still there when the motor's warm, the clutch may need attention. We haven't come across any particular weak points on the driveshafts or wheel bearings, but have a good listen for ticking or whining noises at low speeds and when on full lock.

If you can get to look at them, check the constant velocity (CV) joint boots on all the driveshafts. These are pretty robust but, should one crack, the protective grease will leak out, road muck will get in, and you'll need new CV joints.

If you spot anything amiss with the gearbox, clutch, or any transmission parts, you really have to cost the repairs adequately before even thinking about taking on the vehicle. And don't take someone's word if they are selling a car and said they know how much a particular repair is going to be. Make your own enquiries.

If the repair is the same price they told

*This nice, dry gearbox casing looks in excellent condition*

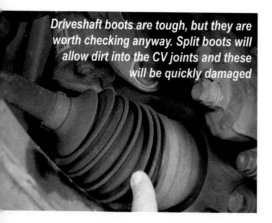

*Driveshaft boots are tough, but they are worth checking anyway. Split boots will allow dirt into the CV joints and these will be quickly damaged*

*Rear differential should also be totally oil-tight, just like this one*

you, all well and good, but don't be surprised if the quote you get is higher. Something like a clutch can take up to five hours to swap, so labour charges can be very high, on top of parts prices that aren't cheap either. Bearing in mind how much choice there is in the Subaru marketplace today, you're better off buying something that's 100 per cent.

## Suspension and steering

When you make a car strong enough to go rallying, it stays the course pretty well when it's only being driven on the road. Imprezas are hardy beasts, and their chassis and underpinnings usually last for ages. However, you should do a thorough visual check to make sure there's no evidence of accident damage or over-enthusiastic driving, such as heavy grounding-out of the underbody or suspension.

The steering is very direct and positive, so any slackness or vagueness noticed is out of character for the car.

Having the correct suspension geometry is vital for the Impreza's good handling and tyre wear, so have a look at all four tyres to make sure they are wearing evenly. If there is uneven wear or bald patches on the tread faces, it could be something as simple as incorrect tyre pressures, but it can signify wheel misalignment, bent suspension or a twisted bodyshell. Obviously sorting out what the problem is essential before committing yourself to the purchase.

## Brakes, wheels and tyres

A quick visual check is needed to make sure the brakes look OK before you go for a drive. A very light coating of rust on the disc faces is acceptable if the car has been parked up for a while (or recently washed), but it should light enough that it will polish off almost as soon as the wheels start turning. Prominent ridges around the disc rims or on the faces are a sign that they are wearing out. Deep scoring of the disc faces is something to be avoided, or haggled over to account for the repair cost.

Fresh imports often have dodgy-looking discs because of the boat trip from Japan but, even so, they should still look smooth under the surface corrosion. Pads should have at least a couple of millimetres of friction material left on them.

On the road the brakes should be powerful and smooth, and pull the car up in a straight line with no tugging to the sides of the road.

If you do agree to take on the car, even subject to it having some work done on the brakes, make sure this waywardness is nothing to do with a damaged chassis (which might show itself if the car persistently turns either way on the road without steering inputs).

Depending on which model you're looking at, the alloy wheels will either still be the factory-fit items, or someone will have already changed them – most likely for something bigger.

Whatever the style of rim, ensure there's no excessive damage from kerbing, and that it's not too corroded.

Check each tyre for wear. The legal tyre wear limit in the UK is 1.6mm across three-quarters of the tread width. Check also that the tyre walls do not have any nicks or cuts from hard kerb contact.

Fitting new tyres might be problematic on a damaged rim, as they may not seal properly.

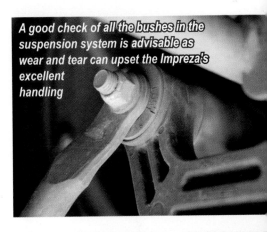

*A good check of all the bushes in the suspension system is advisable as wear and tear can upset the Impreza's excellent handling*

*Check each wheel for scrapes like this. This damage is easily repaired, but a bent or cracked rim will mean a new wheel*

*Very worn rear brakes will soon need replacement discs and pads*

# *What to look for — at a glance*

**Clutch**

With plenty of grip on offer from the awesome four-wheel-drive system, the Impreza's clutch is subject to more stress than vehicles with less traction. Even so, a well cared for example should manage anything up to 45,000 miles before the clutch needs attention

**Electrics**

Typically Japanese and fault-free, but beware any car with upgraded lights. The stock lamps are poor, but their thin wiring won't stand up to larger bulbs or additional spot lights. Additional wiring is needed - make sure it's there

**Interior**

Dull and poor on early cars, but brighter and better made, with better equipment on later cars. Check for undue wear on pedals or gearknob that doesn't line up with the mileage, too. Jap-spec seats are the ones to have, as they are supportive and comfortable. Very sought-after for updating earlier cars, too

**Engine**

Reliable and strong unless badly serviced or poorly tuned, the Impreza's EJ20 boxer motor sounds gruff, but any unexpected mechanical noise should be checked out. Mooing sounds are most likely to come from a faulty dump valve

**Security**

Insurance-approved anti-th measures are going to be vi for getting theft insurance, unless there's something fitt already, budget for adding approved alarm yourself. M cars should have something now, but make sure the releva paperwork is to hand

**Bodywork**

Check for badly-repaired accident damage, and poor paint matches on stonechip refurbishment. On import cars, be sure they've been undersealed to stop the salt worms from biting

LF04 WCK

## Suspension

After a quick visual check for bent or scratched suspension arms listen for knocking and clunking that might indicate worn bushes or mountings that need further investigation. Any damage is likely to be driver-induced

## Transmission

Check for notchy gearchanges and noisy bearings as these will show how healthy the 'box is. Impreza gearboxes are fairly strong, but if they're transmitting much more power than standard, or they've been abused, the life expectancy is shortened. If the clutch bites high on its travel, it's not got much life left

## Check VIN numbers

You will find the model type number and Vehicle Identification Number (chassis number) stamped into a plate in the engine bay. The VIN is also found stamped onto the bodyshell at the engine firewall. The number should agree with that in the car's registration document

## Exhaust

Plenty of Scoobs have performance pipes, so check you can live with the sound. Also make sure that the cats are either still fitted, or that they come with the car when you buy it. You'll need them at MOT time, and they're expensive to buy for one day's use a year!

## Brakes

Check for juddering through the pedal that indicates warped or cracked discs, and look carefully to see how they're wearing. Fade is easy to induce when pressing on, so be warned before you go hurtling around on a test drive

## Wheels and tyres

Check tyres for uneven wear that might signify chassis problems due to misuse or crash damage. Gold wheels are more desirable. Early wheels are less so, and many have already been swapped for bigger rims more in keeping with the car's image and performance

# About the author

Andy Butler has been working with cars all his life. He has been a mechanic, salesman and car stereo consultant, before becoming a specialist motoring writer in 1993.

He has since contributed technical and feature articles to numerous motoring magazines and is the author of four books. He has a particular interest in Japanese cars, and is hailed as the Technical Guru of Japanese Performance magazine.

### Acknowledgements

To David Finch at Subaru UK for the use of various photos used throughout the text. All other photos supplied by Zoë Harrison at ZACE Photographic.

To Paul Watson and Mick Hancock at Vine Place Sports and Performance in Chilton, Co Durham (01388 721122) for letting us take lots of photos of various Scooby details, and for getting in the way in their busy workshop.

To Jonathan McKeary at Performance Subaru in Coleraine (www.performancesubaru.com) for helping decipher Subaru chassis codes.

To Steve Breen and his excellent Impreza website, www.iwoc.co.uk, for providing specification information.

## Ultimate Buyers' Guides include:

Porsche 911SC 1977 to 1983;
ISBN 0 9545579 0 5
Porsche 911 Carrera 3.2 1983 to 1989;
ISBN 0 9545579 1 3
Porsche 911 Carrera (964) 1989 to 1994;
ISBN 0 9545579 3 X
Porsche 911 Carrera, RS & Turbo (993);
ISBN 0 9549990 1 0
Porsche Boxster & Boxster S 1996 to 2005;
ISBN 0 9549990 0 2
Porsche 911 Carrera, Turbo & GT (996)
ISBN 0 9545579 5 6
MGF and TF
ISBN 0 9545579 6 4
Landrover Discovery
ISBN 0 9545579 7 2
Subaru Impreza Turbo
ISBN 09545579 8 0

And watch out for new titles!